Soma Song

Joy Willow

Soma Song

Copyright © 2013 by Joy Willow

All rights reserved. No part of this publication may be reproduced or transmitted in any form or by any means, electronic or mechanical, including photocopy, recording, or any information storage and retrieval system, without permission in writing from the publisher.

Published in the United States by the Word Project Press of Sonora, CA

Requests for permission to make copies of any part of this work should be submitted online at info@wordprojectpress.com

Contact Info
Email: jewillow@sonic.net
Web site: http://www.joywillow.com

Credits:
Cover Image: Joy Willow
Cover Design: Melody Baker
Author Photo: Patricia Harrelson

ISBN: 978-0-9890682-1-5

Library of Congress Control Number: 2013945187

For Janaka -

a unique life of presence,

a faithfulness of loving,

a compass pointing home.

CONTENTS

PROVENANCE
Barrels 3
A Real Valentine 5
Matins at First Light 6
The Cure 8
Provenance 9
The Joy of Riding 11

RIPENING
Leaning into the Wind 15
Racehorse 16
Arting 18
Balancing on Two Feet 20
Two Hands Clapping 21
Sailing Lesson 23

SEEING
Observing Early Fall 27
Eye Contact 29
A Quiet Mind 31
Making Balance 32
Kai 33
Facts, Sentences, and Sayings 35
No Grammar Here 37
The House at the End of the Road 39

IMPERMANENCE
Unwritten Poem 43
Untimely Questions 46
In France, Before Salem 48
At Any Moment 50
Threshold '98 52

Dropping Deeper into Grief 54
It Started with My Feet 55
Disappearing 56
Renting a Bass 57
Practice for Dying 58
Sweet Chocolate Death 59
A Laughing Matter 60
I Hope to Go Gentle 61

CHANGE
Crossing 65
Excavation 67
Word Math 69
R-E-D Star 71
Social Security 72
Absolution 74
The Snake in My Bed 76
Moon Lightning 78

HOME
Grace Notes: (An Invitation to the West) 81
Diving Instructions 82
Note to Self: Saturday Afternoon 83
The Music of Release 85
Singing by Feel 87

SOMA SONG
Sometimes the Breath 91
A Sentient Being Senses 92
Soma Song 93

PROVENANCE

Barrels

Once I slept in a wine barrel.
It was big enough for a bed,
a chest of drawers,
a lamp, and a chair.
I could peer out tiny windows,
or gaze at feathery pines above the skylight.

On weekend retreat made for dozing and dreaming
cradled in the barrel's womb,
I slept with the musk of old wine filling my nostrils…
I dreamt of underground cellars
where Celtic harp and candlelight
wove a magical spell among rows of barrels,
a cool dampness invited dancing,
a Sonoma County gathering
in the Valley of the Moon.

They say that a good-sized barrel
can house a family of six.
Smaller barrels become furniture,
or grow tomatoes on a back deck,
or hold a mailbox.

Yet these staves of bent wood
are made for holding the essence of grape,
lending flavors and textures of oak;
holding until the moment of tap,
the moment of readiness,
the moment of breath.

Then the rivers of joy are poured
from the alchemical vats
into a thirsty, anxious world,
eager to celebrate this moment.

I slept in a wine barrel once.
It was a time of rest and restraint.
It was a time of waiting,
and slow, delicious seasoning.

A Real Valentine

Feel the gap
    between the molecules,
Taste the untouchable space,
    that emptiness so full
Of electric power
    that we are propelled onward
To the next arising
    as surely as day follows night.

Feeling for the gap
    between the molecules,
Clears the mind
    re-setting the compass
To the central happiness,
    a forever moment of the heart
Never found
    on a greeting card.

The gap is a warm invitation
    from a familiar unknown place,
A release into solid joy
    moving like a river to ocean's embrace:
Being the gap
    between the molecules,
Allows us to breathe, sit tall,
    enjoy the view.

Matins at First Light
(for Cheddars)

The prelude and preparation
For my morning meditation
With the rising sun
Is to watch, from a distance
So as not to intrude,
The daily feline ritual
That takes place in a
Carefully chosen area
Out among the fallen oak leaves,
Or in the garden's redwood mulch,
Or at the base of a specific manzanita.
The early chill necessitates my vigilance
For he will not dally in the cold.

He approaches carefully,
Head bent low like an aging priest,
Entering his sacred space
Marked off by precision, scent, and habit.

Then a patient, yet urgent search begins.
A search for the holy of holies.
Turning, testing, sniffing,
And turning again
Until the perfect spot is selected
As repository for today's offering.

He sits statue-still,
Weight on front legs
As if about to kneel in prayer.
With eyes tightly closed he offers up his tithe,
A sacrament of excrement,
A blessing to the earth.

A ripple rides up his spine
Followed by a small tremor,
Then a sudden flurry of rotations and half-circles,
Incessant pawings and reachings and roundings
Until the gift is concealed
And completely covered.
Then with a quick shake of a hind leg
The liturgy is over
And he is done.

Yet tomorrow he will know exactly
Where to repeat these rites
In their exact proportions and
With equal ceremony.
Whereas to the human eye
The daily donation is totally hidden
And anonymous,
Unlike with those Protestant dogs
Who have lost the sense of ritual altogether
And leave their steaming masses
Out in the open – anywhere at all!
Not so the Catholic cat
Fastidious devotee of crepuscular customs
And modest reverences.

Finally, after earnest, repetitious cleansing,
He tucks his paws under him,
Settling in beside me,
As we sit together,
A congregation of two,
Meditating on the revelation
Of the new day.

The Cure

They've all diagnosed it this way over the years:
"Yin deficient."
A condition arising from false yang excess,
the "doing" sickness of "I," "me," "mine," and "mind."

So at long last having seen
the beauty and the benefit,
indeed, the art of consistently doing nothing,
slowly learning that this art is the cure,
and staying curious the path
to the fire of creation and true yang energy.

So. Ah, this amazing art
of not-doing
of wu-wei (without effort)
of via negativa
of neti-neti (not this, not that);
these are beautiful negations
pointing to the watery dark,
the place of light's birth
and the space of spontaneous arisings.

It begins with nothing at all.
It continues with less and less.
Wise ones say: "When in doubt, don't."
So simple.
Just waiting in stillness…
watching it all arise!

Provenance

The leaf falls only once to the ground.

There is no repeating
This exact trajectory.
The movements of cloud, snowflake and pebble
Create imaginary lines of passage
With no imitation.

Our habits of morning,
Our routines of work,
Schedules of waking and sleeping
Are never identical
Though illusion would deceive.

However rehearsed and explicit,
The motions of the ballet are unique,
Their internal movements
Cannot be absolutely recalled.

However precisely traced,
The dark glass of memory
Dims past actions
And prevents capture.

There is evolution and sequencing
In the spiral patterns of growth,
Layering and sediment
In the maturity of form;
There is turn and curl
In the design of activity
Rooted in rest.

A short walk
Around the block
Proves directly
That nothing is ever the same twice.

The leaf falls to the ground only once.

The Joy of Riding

In this moment, the question:
Is there discipline enough
To drop ever deeper
Into pleasure?

Waiting for my favorite horse at the stable
There is easy patience:
Knowing how its body will feel beneath me,
Knowing how secure the seat,
Anticipating the sweet and swift communication
From lightly balanced reins,
An animal communion laced with moisture
And electrical charge,
An easy connection,
A gentle focus,
Merging time, rhythm, and space…

Thus I am tethered to the breath
Surrendering joyfully
To the ride of my life

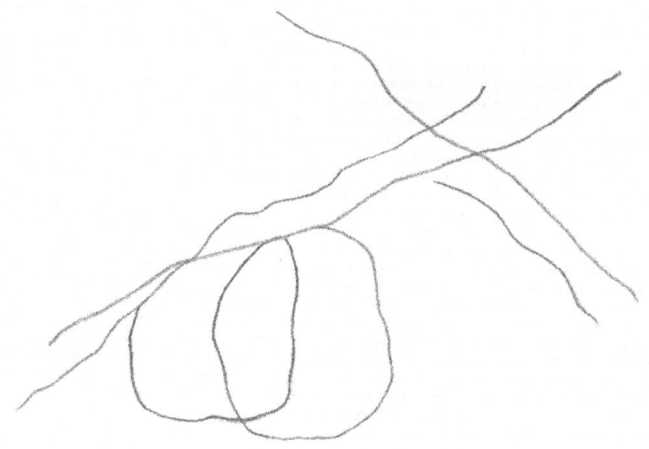

RIPENING

Leaning Into the Wind

    Flying dark grey bodyrobe,
      Silver wings folded back vibrating
        In the streaming air,
          White face leading eagerly
            She leans horizontal into the wind
              For balance

    A witch, an angel, a nun
      With habit blowing back, wings
        Using the past as fuel
          For the turning wheel of power

    Wings of dual existence
      Folding and unfolding
        In movements of grace,
          Systole and diastole
            Pumping songs of truth
              And the heart's confidence

    Her trajectory builds speed
      Through layers of darkness and light,
        Letting go into the fluid details of the day
          By constant flight adjustments
          And tiny listenings,
            Increasing momentum, skill,
            And elevation

    She leans into the wind.
      She goes where it's hot.
        Unafraid.

Racehorse

He trains, he rests, he walks, he eats,
He sleeps while standing still.

He knows love's disciplines
And the embrace of muscle,
The fire in its fibers,
The power of the heartpump.

But the games of chance and fortunes gambled,
The pressures of winning and the echoes of will,
These are left unrecognized, for he has no name
And nothing to defend nor gain.

He trains, he rests, and knows not why,
He knows no prize nor plan,
Only the purity of sweat and hay
And moonlight's soothing hand.

The simple act of running to the limit of one's strength,
The testing of endurance and the pleasure in the stretch,
He trains, he rests, he walks, he eats,
He sleeps while standing still.

A horse without name
A monk in his cell
He sees beyond the narrow stall,
He sees beyond with his large moist eye
And knows the heart's intention.

He sees, he trains, he rests, he runs
And waits upon the day,
He cannot fail, for he is he
And happy with no name;
He smells the wind, he rolls in grass,
He knows the rhythms in his feet,
For he is he
And seeing is,
And training is his life.

He walks, he rests, each day the same,
He is a horse without a name;
He sleeps while standing still.

Arting

Making art is not a making at all.
It is stripping away
All layers of clothes:
Coats of fear,
Robes of pride,
Boots of ambition,
Hats of compulsion,
Jewels of fantasy,
Belts of manipulation,
Collars of agenda,
Undergarments of doubt.

All layers dropped to the floor.
Now naked,
Completeness is felt
Moving in the materials,
Moving in the body,
One movement of infinite variation
And unified structure.

There is waiting.
Openness.
Breathing.
No thoughts about what to do,
No thoughts about how to do,
No thoughts about what is next,
No thoughts about how is this,
No thoughts about rules or time,
No thoughts save those woven
Into the great mind of feeling.

Clinging mind clothed in the rough fabric of normalcy
Cannot capture, repeat, nor even recall the movements,
Sounds, nor colors of the dance.

There is only an echo of remembered texture.
Perhaps.
Yet this emptiness is the price of ecstasy.

Balancing on Two Feet

She holds a circle, a quiet space, a whole embrace,
she is an open freeway
just waiting for your truck;
she sees it all as rest.

He travels inside the circle,
covering the territory like Johnny Appleseed,
flying like Superman,
striding like Lewis and Clark,
burrowing like Bin Laden,
all the while reciting every word known to man;
he sees it all as movement.

Both sphere and axis are needed to spin this globe,
a marshmallow on a stick,
a bead on a necklace,
a fish on a bicycle;
both can live as one, in one.

And like a pink flamingo,
one can balance on one leg,
and the other leg;
this gets easier with practice.
Or one can just balance on two feet;
this too gets easier with practice.

She holds a circle;
he travels inside the circle.
Both can live as one, in one.
This gets easier with practice.

Two Hands Clapping

When did applause begin?
A plausible explanation may be

that early man observed primates
as they excitedly beat their chests;

perhaps we learned from them
two thumps for "yes," one thump for "no,"

perhaps we added the hands
clapping vigorously together

appreciating ["yes, yes"] a tasty bonebroth
or the story of a well-executed hunt;

and surely it was useful to discover
that predators scurried away

from the sharp, sudden
thunder of clapping.

Around the campfire
songs of call and answer

may well have included hands,
bones and stones;

with the aid of a rich brew, our strict meters
exploded into a riotous rhythmic finale!

The light applause of leaves
in the winter winds,

the secret games of children
clap-talking their invented patterns,

a concert of applause was carried
by hand, around the world, rotating like clouds.

We were conceived in appreciation, the soft clap
of sperm and egg connecting,

the union of right hand, male
with the left hand, female.

The right hand of Jesus says, "love one another"
the left hand of Jesus says, "there is no death" [CLAP]

The right hand of Buddha says,
"everything is interconnected"

The left hand of Buddha says,
"nothing is permanent" [CLAP]

The right hand of your father says, "get a job"
the left hand of your mother says, " eat your soup" [CLAP]

What is the sound of two hands clapping?
Put your own right hand together with your left hand:

Applaud yourself
and hear what you have to say.

Sailing Lesson

The skipping stone hits the highpoints
then is gone.

The boat lives in these waters,
knows the ebb tide's dip and stall,
and rides the flow's return.

The speedy pebble can only skim the surface,
then sink.

Pain and fear of pain,
loss and fear of loss
have flung me far across the deep…

That ancient urge to drop away
arises with its luring pull
and tempts me to avoid the squalls.

I aim to be a boat,
an aware little eye, open in all weathers
stormy or serene.

I aim to tend my craft,
learn the compass of compassion,
and navigate the unknown.

SEEING

Observing Early Fall

Look, just now—
Bronze stillness
Amphitheater of oaks
Holding their breath in twilight's turning
Ecstasy of graceful death
And grand decay.

See, there—
Pewter atmosphere
Stage of sky
Indecisive in a changing season
Muted grey questions
And smoky wisps.

Behold—
Amber shadows
Corridors of coolness
Casting darkened layers of leaves
Inky blots spilled on wavy hills
And folded fields.

See, ah—
Silvery flash
Dance-floor of rumblings
Rainfall practicing for the months ahead
Relief and shine
And grateful mouths.

Oh, look—
Crystalline morning
Platters of sunshine
Slanting and slicing through haze
Sparkling daylight knock-out engagement ring
And promise of things to come.

Eye Contact

The black hole
At the center of galaxies
Is reflected perfectly
At the center of our eyes.
Diving into this blackness
We enter the mystery
Of seeing.

A kaleidoscope of colors,
The limbic iris swirls
Around the dark gate
Which grows larger
As it softens,
Swallowing more,
And even more reality.

Yet somewhere beyond, within,
A new world is born
From a dilating
Universal cervix,
Perfect circle of ebony light,
Singular identical point
Unifying all mankind.

The pupil is schooled
In disciplines of illumination,
Recording time's presence in memory,
Yet never fixing the moment
Nor stealing the soul's movement
In the beautiful lie
Of an ordinary camera.

Turn now and gaze
For the next half minute
Into someone's eyes.
Dive into this blackness;
Enter the mystery
At the center
Of seeing.

A Quiet Mind

To dwell silently
In the fullness of the moment,

To listen to the lark and the dove
As they converse across the copse,

To feel the deepening shadows
Like a cloak gradually drawn closer
Around the shoulders,

To know the simplicity of evening
When the sun dips low and the scent of burnt hay
Rises from the ground,

To stop the wheel for a little moment
And, with an easy heart, notice
The disappearance of want.

Now see the sudden shaft of light
Glittering on those few new leaves
At the end of an arching branch of oak.

Making Balance

Why does man fall back
In a pale green and delicate yellow drowse
Upon the sweet-scented grass
At the quickening of the year?
Yet when time closes for the endless
Sleepy trance of dormancy,
We leap and cheer and feel the blood speed
Singing through living limbs!

Perhaps Spring completely rules
And all we can do
Is lie back and marvel;
Perhaps we try to save the falling world
By pouring out encouragement
Into the dying air.

Kai
(for Kai Kellerman)

Let me be your keel,
Your rudder and rock,
Your compass and star;
Let me steady your sail
When winds howl
And waters rise up;
When the sands swirl about your shifting feet
Let me offer an arm, and ear, a word, a tear,
A simple cup of tea.

Let me be your keel
Your rudder and rock,
Let me live beneath your house
And trace your footfalls with a magnet and net
Lest the floor weaken beneath you;
Let time expand inside you while you lie sleeping,
Let me be your rest.

Let me be your sherpa
Through labyrinths of decision,
Through unforeseen countries,
Through gates of destiny and allure;
Let me safeguard your dream
So that upon awaking, you may sing the praises
Of your own creative Self;
Let me show you all the glory hidden inside
The illusions and dung heaps of this world.

For that day shall come
When eyes shall fully open and see:
You yourself are keel,
Rudder and rock,
With a true compass
In your deeply listening heart.

Facts, Sentences, and Sayings

(*with thanks to Harrison Ford, the AARP Magazine,
Janaka, Brother Steindl-Rast, Arjuna Ardagh, and many
menopausal women*)

   Who is saying sayings?
   Maybe sayings say themselves onward and forever!

*More people are kicked to death by mules
Than die in aviation accidents worldwide.*

If spilled cereal stays on the floor
For more than five seconds
It must be thrown away.

*Contemplation of mortality
Can bring on a mellow mood.*

   Who is saying sayings?
   Maybe sayings say themselves onward and forever!

There is no such thing as changing the subject.
The subject is one, immutable, and unchanging.

I peed on the ground outside a tent with a lot of people.
I expect this has been going on for many centuries.

Use it or lose it. (Now there's a saying!)

   Who is saying sayings?
   Maybe sayings say themselves onward and forever!

There is no such thing as a quiet mind.
We just get as close as we can.

Forget trying to pry open that part of your brain
That is so shut like a gate.

The cure for exhaustion is not rest.
The cure for exhaustion is wholeheartedness.

   Who is saying sayings?
   Maybe sayings say themselves onward and forever!

Use it or lose it—yes, every little moment is used
To weave completion to the day.
No matter how mundane or bothersome.

This is what sayings say.
When all together.

You are poetry itself.
You are loved.
This is what sayings say.
Even if in code.

No Grammar Here

At her desk
With freshly sharpened pencil,
The fourth-grader bends eagerly
To the curious task of labeling
Subjects and verbs,
Circling prepositional phrases,
Marking modifiers, parsing
Conjunctions and exclamations.
(After all, this is grammar school.)
And like a careful archeologist
She separates and analyses,
Discovering the thrills
Of linguistic structure.

But wait. She senses
That lightning strikes,
Steam rises,
Cats purr,
And arms reach out
From a gathering
Of invisible activity
With subject and verb inseparable.
She sees that the thing
Is what it does,
And does what it is!

How strange that names can carry truth
Yet also imply their opposite:
Ocean – no ocean.
Me – no me.
You – no you.
God – no God.
When so defined

Things just seem to cancel each other out.
Maybe "things" aren't really things at all,
But energies appearing and disappearing
Like magic,
Like breathing.
Without clear edges.

The child learns to speak a language of locality –
This is here, that is there.
She learns the rules of writing
And the craft.

The poet uses words to point
Beyond the words,
Beyond the prison of the sentence
And the confines of syntax.
She uses grammar fluently,
Yet knows there can be
No grammar here.

The House at the End of the Road

Dried sunflowers and sagging jasmine
nearly conceal the deserted birdhouse
supported by a rusty pole;
a few remnants of paint
still cling to the little nesting place,
its one voiceless tenant
a magnolia branch needing support.

Down the overgrown path
is a small house and tool shed,
both slowly being swallowed
by a tangle of vines and weedy grass.
The top half of the shed's door
hangs tenuously on one hinge.

Tony kept the clapboard exterior
painted a crisp white
until he died two decades ago;
his widow comes now and then
to prune around the cement Madonnas,
or wash the enormous windows
that made the house the perfect studio
with perfect light.
Tony was an artist,
although no one saw his work.
Rumor has it he painted the light itself
with brushes from Paris.

From the road one could see
The two of them together, their wide windows
Never shrouded with curtains;

One could see them bent over the current project,
laughing, backlit and bathed
in a silvery glow.

No one knew what they did there.
Rumor has it the paintings were invisible
to the living,
only seen by the dying.
Perhaps Tony died
so he could finally see his work
with his own eyes;
perhaps the house is not for sale
because the work is not yet done.

Marie herself is now the brush
That continues moving with keen delight;
though she is nearly ninety
her vision is unclouded.
From the road she can be seen
clearing the overgrown path,
refurbishing the birdhouse;
the feathered ones are drawn to her humming
that old song of her youth,
the one about joys and pains of love,
its French lyrics weaving in and out of her mind
like a tender breeze.

Marie visits whenever she can
To put the final touches on the painting
now becoming visible,
a painting of the house
at the end of the road.

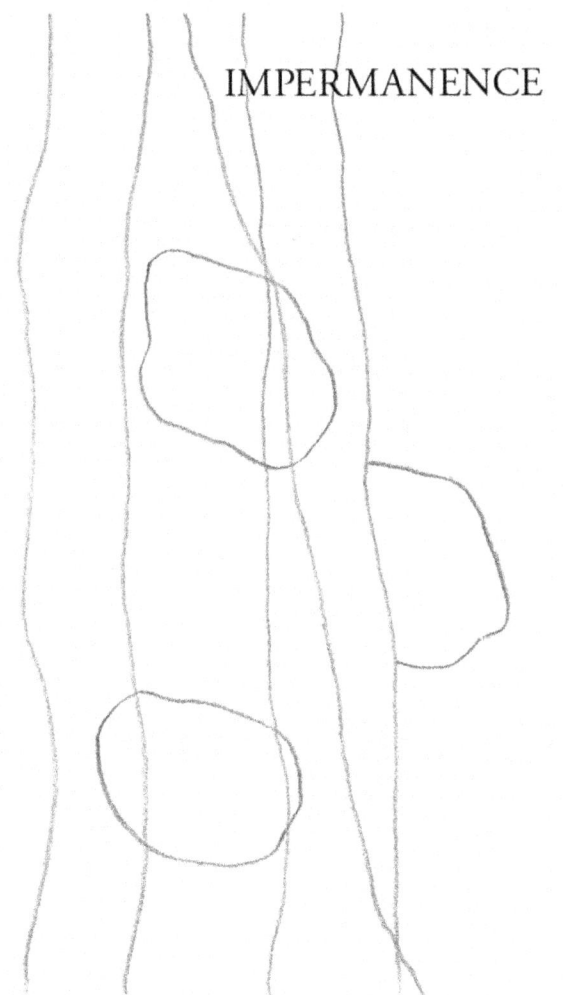
IMPERMANENCE

Unwritten Poem

I want to write a poem
About the end of the world,
About the end of recorded time
At least according to the Mayans;
About the stillness of solstice
And falling off the cliff of what used to be
Solid ground.

I will write this poem
Unless stopped by a shooter
Randomly projecting his neurosis
Onto innocent ones
Going about their day
At the end of the world;
Or unless stalled by a malfunction
Of some vital organ,
Or unless hit by a bus.

Can I write this poem
About the downfall of civilization,
The collapse of verbal communication,
Common sense and caring?
Can I document a distracted society,
Shaking with addiction's tremors,
Staring into the eyes of its own demons,
Its own projected panic?

Can I footnote this poem with references
To the literature of symbols
And the technology of the sacred,
All the keys, graphs, and maps
That got us here to this day
When it was – all of it –
Predicted to end?

In the dark hours before dawn I lie very still,
On my back, hands folded across my heart,
And listen carefully and long
For the softest whimper that signals the sound
Of the last day of the world.

Instead I hear broken voices reporting
Gunshot rampages ricocheting around the world;
I hear the wailing of women and children
As they cower and scatter like deer.

The bang and the whimpering are both heard
Throughout these longest nights.

Stop.
Enough.
The world cannot continue this way.

As the earth turns from new moon to full,
As the baby suckles his mother's breast,
As young cattle romp and feed in fertile pastures,
As the fires of winter burn old wood
And warm our frozen hands,
As the snow blankets the brown fields,
As we lie still in the December night,
Hands folded across our hearts,
Perhaps if we are quiet enough
We can feel the waters breaking,
The drawing together that signals delivery
Through the labyrinth of agony,
Pushing forth a new being,
A new world,
Its round head just beginning to crest,
Its first cries already in the air,

Its eyes still closed to the brilliant translucence
That awaits its arrival.

No, I cannot write a poem about the failing of the world;
But I can listen attentively
And welcome that which is arising.

Untimely Questions

What is going on here?
Is creative living a liability?

Why couldn't Plath resolve the Daddy issue?
Why couldn't van Gogh sell a painting?
Why box the ears of a boy
Whose name was Beethoven?
Or any boy for that matter.
Why a vocal hemorrhage for Caruso?

What is going on here?

Why would Isadora be strangled by her scarf?
Why should Fritz Wunderlich trip on shoelaces
And tumble the marble stairs?
Why couldn't Schumann compose his way to health?
Why walk into the sea, Virginia?

What is going on here?

Why a beautiful actress, decapitated?
Why couldn't Michael learn to sleep?
Why didn't rehab work for Whitney
And countless others?
Why gun down Lennon in his prime?
Why were Schubert and Mozart dead by thirty-three?
And Keats by twenty-six....

Why? What?
What is going on here?

Perhaps when the creative life is
Unacknowledged, unappreciated,
Or manipulated for profit,
The container becomes a pressure cooker of obsession
With yet more success, more love,
Envy, comparison, and looking good.
The body rebels.
The mind fractures.

 Or perhaps we will never know.

In France, Before Salem

I climbed the ladder to the platform.
They untied the rope from around my waist.
A moment of relief, but soon it was worse.
They used the rope to tie my wrists to a pole.
It felt like my arms were being cut off,
But then they went numb.

I choked from the smoke. Nearly passed out.
I felt my dress on fire, then my underdress.
Then the platform shook and I heard the sound
Of a thousand crows.

Suddenly I was flying above the insane crowd….
Really flying, not just pretend!
I watched it all like a dream.
Was I dreaming?
Would I wake up at five o'clock in the morning,
Dress quickly by the light of the late moon,
And hurry down to the kitchen to begin the baking?

I don't think this is a dream.
This fire seemed to arise on its own. From nowhere.
Yet the forces that made it were brewing for a long time.
Smoldering coals of fear and suspicion were ignited
By opinion and ignorance,
Rumor and righteousness,
The sparks blown through the village
Like dust devils in the street.

Oh, my goodness! Somehow I can see my little brother
Playing behind the house.

Oh, I guess I will not be learning to swim this summer
In the cool lake.

At Any Moment

We are ridiculously close
To dying
At any moment.

The heart could attack,
The neck snap,
The brain could stroke,
The foot slip,
The car crash
At any moment.

Bombs could fall,
Bullets tear,
Buildings collapse
At any moment.

A strange fear arises with this knowing --
Disturbing sleep with a nameless anxiety;
In the middle of a crowded theatre
It bursts through the door, blazing terror;
In the middle of breakfast
There it is on television,
The latest horror.

Lives move in and out of form
With slow windings and swift suddenness.
There is resistance to these constant changes.
We call them "loss."

The grim reaper is the picture of this fear.
He is created out of old cloth, rusty metal,
And mental cobwebs.
He is static, cartoonish, made of dust.

Tales of doom and destruction
Elicit shrieks of delight.
Perhaps because we can smell the lie
In these images.
Just shadows on a wall.
The whole catastrophe
Just shadows on a wall.

Lives move in and out of form
With slow windings and swift suddenness.

Perhaps we could live more easily with this --
Remembering kindness and simple affection
Go a long way toward soothing anxious hearts.
When things go bump in the night
How quickly a gentle touch
Can restore the purring
In the timid cat.

Lives move in and out of form
With slow windings and swift suddenness.
And like the cat we can be alert and vigilant,
Yet purring peacefully;
Even though at any moment
Forms alter and shift,
Decay and disappear
With slow winding turns of fortune
And swift movements of fate.

The sharp edge
Of any moment,
The only place
To actually dance
With the shadows
On the wall.

Threshold '98
(for Charles Hoy Steele)

I knew just when
You would choose to pass.
You were speechless,
Lying so very still.
Yet I had the surety of migrating birds
That your flying day
Was seven more.
Then it would be new moon
And Fall Equinox
And Rosh Hashanah
At once.
A Sunday.

It was a sunny day.
Hot.
I dressed in white and black.
So did your mother.
Not our custom.
White butterflies gathered on the lawn.
Easily a hundred in close congregation.
Burning candles created a blanket of fragrance
Under which our collective breath suspended
And slowed
Along with yours.
Snake and lizard rose from the earth
And entered the dry house.
The dog lay under your bed.
She also knew.
All the women in your life gathered around
Gazing at your translucent cheekbones.
You were a quiet gravity of light.
The guardian stray cat passed with you.

We covered you with rose petals and precision.
The electricity failed.

Later, at midnight,
Your bed became a ship with three sails,
And all around the house an otherworldly commotion
Of entrances and exits
Kept me from sleep.
Yet resting with you
In these latter days
Was so complete,
That sleeping and eating were unnecessary.

We sailed together to the edge of the world.
Then you tipped your Greek fisherman's hat
And were gone.
Gone past the horizon in a flash of light.
We parted here
At the edge of time.
At the threshold.
I remained on the shore
And drank water.

Your fragrance dissolved into all the elements
Like homeopathic tincture,
Like salve for wounds.
You became part of a choreography of healing.

I remained on the shore
And drank water.

Dropping Deeper into Grief

Dropping deeper into grief
   Into the underworld descending,
     Wearing the dress of dark ash

Falling, naturally, into deepest earth,
   Trails of water leeching away all agitation

Dropping deeper into grief,
   The grief of animals,
     Centuries-old sorrow of creatures and cliffs,
       Of dry leaves and crawling mists

Rooting down further still into darkness
   Away from all light, harsh or beautiful,
     Away from hours, roads, ambitions,
       And the glare of haste

Away from all but this free-falling
   Into the warm, swollen belly of life

Supported only by the emptiness
   That knows how to caress
     The sadness of hearts

It Started With My Feet

It started with my feet.
They were like yours.
My eyes were closed, but I knew
Exactly how your feet felt to you.

Then the hands.
My fingers grew thicker,
My hands and forearms heavier.
They were yours.

For several months after you left
The sensation of you was literal in me,
At first frightening
Then a welcome gift.

You came in feet first.
Then legs, knees, hips, trunk.
All were you.
A curious communion and unique.
In your company I was comforted.

I found no explanation
In the books on grief.
But we had joked
About a signal or sign.

This was better than something falling off the shelf.
This was better than anything we could have imagined.
Thank you.

Disappearing

Internal sun
Orb of warm white radiance
Reveals the next step.

Internal sun
Met with a certain
Patient curiosity
Reveals unfolding
Expression.

Beginning as image
It spreads and swallows
Whole;
Skin boundary disappears
Vibrational space,
Suspension
And awareness.

And when that grainy, craven hunger comes,
At twilight or on weekend holidays,
To stop and sink and feel this disappearing
Throughout the body's scope,
And know it as a common thing;
To yield without condition or delay,
Without shame nor masking shame,
Complete surrender to whatever this is.

We are visible and invisible at once;
The next step is clearly seen
In the light of
This internal sun.

Renting a Bass
(for Janaka)

I imagined renting a bass,
A tall, upright
Mahogany mellow bass
Just like yourself;

I imagined standing it
In the corner of your room
To surprise you
On your next visit;

I imagined your long brown fingers
Gently touching the pliant strings
For the first time
In forty years;

I imagined you and your bass
Standing next to my baby grand,
The rich soft sounds
Making easy, polite introductions.

I imagined us dropping deep
Into the well of music, listening
Sharing silence as we pulley up wooden ladles
Overflowing with cool, sweet water.

I imagine us filling space
With the electric communion of loving –
Fingers or no fingers,
Bass or no bass.

Practice for Dying

It actually happens quite often,
this sensate vanishing:

A complete silence.
an utter lack of visual stimulation.
No smell, no taste, no touch –
not even the sense of bodily weight, pressure,
shape, or contact points.

Just a vanishing.

It begins with hands, spine, or feet
then spreads, luminous and quicksilver;
a vanishing so enchanting –
like flying at impossible velocity!

There is still awareness but without body sensations;
full consciousness here and everywhere at once.

Is this practice for dying?
Is this what it is like?

If so, sign me up.

Sweet Chocolate Death

Sometimes we want that death,
that peace and pitch blackness
that acts like a drug
and drags us to sleep;

Sometimes we crave that death,
that rest from the drama,
constant change and
constant projections of
image and story and threat;

Sometimes we need that death,
like we need chocolate
and God.
Yes, we do, in spite of being
hard-wired for survival.

All of that over-amped fear
is the wiring's kit for survival,
a kit with no chocolate,
a kit whose purpose is to scare us away
from our true survival
and sweetness unwrapped.

A Laughing Matter

Death is no laughing matter.

Or is it?

When face to face with the one and only
human inevitability
What the hell else is there to do?
Cry?
If we take away gravity,
Crying looks an awful lot like laughing.
And most all other actions become quite pointless.

A rich, perfect laugh involves the viscera,
An incarnation and incorporation of light:
Muscles signal a lack of decorum,
A lack of control,
A release from effort
And an end to all worry.
The body lets go.
The mind lets go.
A sane and spontaneous response,
We can laugh ourselves all the way to eternity.

Laughing is a shared secret,
An answer to every known koan:
HA!

I Hope To Go Gentle
(with apologies to Dylan Thomas)

I hope to go gentle
Into that good night,
And gracefully dance
With the dying light;

And if I rage, forgive me
For my poor heart has tried
To untie the attachments
Of blind love and hunger:
I have tried by turning
And the practice of turning
Towards the quiet seat
And the practice of sitting,
With patient hands,
With silent tongue,
With open eyes,
Sitting and sitting,
Turning and turning…
Towards silence.

Yes, I hope to go gentle
Into this good life,
Be it glorious day
Or darkest night.

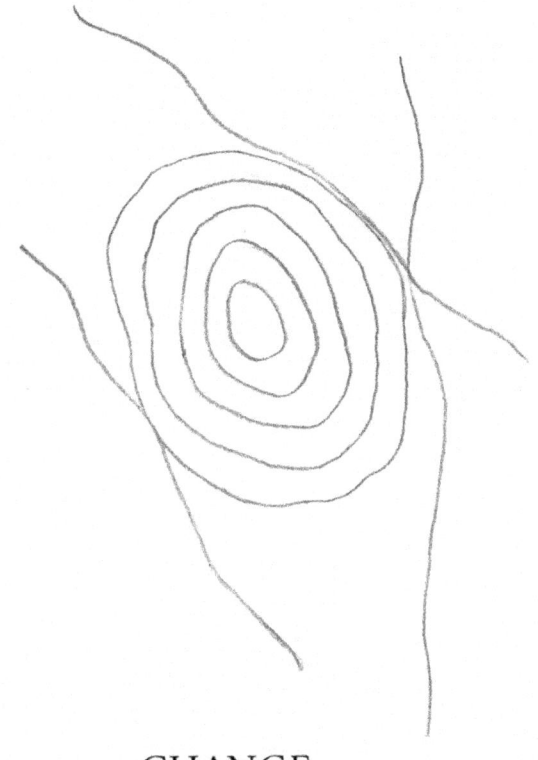

CHANGE

Crossing

The American poet, Auden, said of Yeats:
"Proud Ireland hurt you into poetry."

What calamity, what emergency or loss
"Hurts" the poet into that urgent quest
For lines of sustenance?
What sudden or sustained concern
Has us writing in the wee hours?
What has us walking the road
Before anyone is awake,
Exhaling anxiety into phrases of sensibility,
Inhaling the soothing cold of morning's declaration?

Sometimes pain will push us into poetry,
Helping us balance on the living blade
That cuts between an ordered life
And chaos;
Yet sometimes we pick up the pen,
Having released the hold on fear,
And notice something else is stirring,
Healing us into poetry.

Then the written word points to our own walkway
And beyond
Where we can see both the footprints left behind,
Indelible sentences completed,
As well as the steps under us just now,
Feeling all twenty-eight bones of our feet
Rolling toward future stanzas.

Poetry then accompanies us
Across that old suspension bridge of rope,
Where the way is narrow as a line
And breath the balance beam of hope;
High above the dark abyss
Riveted to the here and now,
We make this crossing step by step
An ecstatic bard with drunken song and crazy bow;
We mutter lyrics and scribble in the air
Healing words lived out-loud,
Words that vanish
Like the clouds.

Excavation

Peeling the layers of a life;
Uncovering the construction of a psyche:

First an exfoliation
Of obvious dead skin--
Easy work, shining results;

Then more tedious tasks of
Sensing, removing, examining
Separate layers of separation,
Isolate particles of darkness,
Conglomerate areas that need a pick ax,
A layer of muscle,
A layer of nerve,
Evidence of waste, fur, tooth and whisker,
Constant slow erosion of the comforting
And the familiar,
Relentless digging which now can't be stopped….

But here we are, deep in earth's discovery grave,
The sounds of daily life receding into the distance.

Perhaps we will find the 7,000 year-old
Carbon-dated bones
And perhaps succeed in living close to the bone,
Stripped to essence.
Wrist bone flexed carrying water.
Shin bone split chopping wood.
Hip and spine intact.
Perhaps we will celebrate this find
And emerge to join the animate world.

Or perhaps we will stay down here and wait:
Wait in the queue,
Wait for the end,
Wait for the waters to flow,
For the change
That will surely come.

Word Math

the
the simple
the simple truth
the bare bones essence
the language of formula
the crystalline clarity
the obvious
"le mot juste"
simple
not complicated
'tho infinitely complex

the search for what is right in front of us
like fractals
a simple process of reduction
repeated over and over
yields not vanishing into thin air
but the intricacy of the natural world,
the art of cubism,
the broken and Baroque lines of Bach,
a polyphony of sounds that defy gravity,
the soaring dance of trees in a rainforest
each taking an intended position as in the ballet
first position – the
second position – the simple
third position – the simple truth
the language of equation
the lyricism of song lines
the waves of warp and weft
all strung out and woven together,
a fabric of existence
strong and colorful and infinitely varied

one plus one plus one
minus one minus one
subtractions and divisions
create additions and multiplication

love always exists
even in the deepest pit
even in the slightest fragment
creation uses the breaking apart,
the disintegration,
for new forms, new integration, repeating cycles
all crashing together in space ... marvelously

R-E-D Star

Cold darkening of eventide,
sky completely overcast
except for one small bright blue star
twinkling like mad outside my window,
its light only now seen
long, long after it has died;

In this dimming of day
I see clearly that I am a red star,
Retired and Extremely Dangerous,
still shining
still viable
still powerful
loaded
ready
still.

Social Security

What is secure about society?
What is permanent about people?

Humans stammer a language of division
When right outside the door
Nature is humming a song of completeness.

We are solitary creatures,
Born alone, dying alone,
Experiences that are ours alone.
As infants we are fully content
With self-generated sounds and movements,
With the play of shadows and light,
With the layered symphony of calls and twittering
From unseen creatures.
Until some need moves us to cry out,
We are happy alone in our world.
Until we are taught social skills,
And learn to relate and desire a tribe.
Then this cup of familiar brew is laced
With a powerful spike of hormones
Which will drive us right through the next several decades.
Which will drive us until we open the door,
Take a long, slow walk,
Amazed that we could have feared
And forgotten this delicious aloneness.
Not every warm summer moon needs to be shared!

Many who outlive mates
Will contribute their stories of separation
As well as their tales of awakening.
There is a hunger for this wisdom.
And so we willingly support
The drift into age, sending the message:
Elders are still a valued part of the tribe.

Aloneness and society, like yin and yang,
Do a spiral dance
Leaving a paper trail
For future generations.

Absolution

One hot September night
during that two week period
when my husband and mother both passed,
I made a small, tentative journey downtown with my sister.
I hadn't been outside the house in many days.
It felt like years.
We took a little detour –
to the carwash.

I put the car in neutral;
the dark, oblong box of a building took us in.
I felt trapped, vulnerable,
unable to escape.
Suddenly we were being water-boarded
with forceful cascading deluge
and assaulted by the deafening roar
of menacing machinery.

Would it stop if I confessed
to not having exercised
or eaten in a while? Or if I admitted aloud,
right now, that my house hadn't been cleaned recently?
Those long metal arms overhead
didn't seem too receptive.
I needed to return home immediately.

I closed my eyes and tried to relax.
"Hey, it's Saturday night," my sister noted.
"Yes, and here we are, out on the town," I replied.
The carwash was just the first thrilling step
before Whole Foods.

Slowly we began to giggle until our laughter
drowned out the demon pelting us with soap.
I gazed at the iridescent suds,
aqua blue, pink, with a touch of gold
as they slid down the windshield.
We laughed all the way through
the digital clock of the air dry.
We drove away smiling, clean,
and ready for the world.

The Snake in My Bed

There is a snake in my bed.
It appears when needing to start its contractions
And shed skin.

There is a snake in my bed
Whose body becomes the winding road
I walk along through a town being remodeled
From crumbling hillside foundations.

I walk with a purpose
That keeps changing;
I can only guess.

  A man on horseback follows me,
  Magically appearing and disappearing;
  A man with the power to call forth.

Suddenly the road drops away,
Straight down a steep slope
To a stream below
Flowing with purest water.
Straight down I fly,
Carried on the wind,
My open prayer hands in front of me
Holding a ball of light,
Holding still through this
Tunnel of rushing air.

Landing in the cold stream
I wade over slippery rocks
And contemplate the climb ahead
On the uphill side.

Contemplate how slowly and carefully
I must proceed...
Shedding extra clothing, weight,
And questionable habits,
Moving forward half-naked and unencumbered.
Moving forward with careful hand-holds,
Each rock ledge and clump of vegetation
A welcome gift.

       The man on horseback
       Appears to be at the top
       Already.

Slowly upward I crawl and slither
Feeling damp earth and smooth stone
Against my bare skin.

Feeling my way along, meandering,
Stopping to rest on a sunny rock.
Yet I am called forth
With encouraging whispers --
Whispers from the small blue heart
Of the snake
In my bed.

Moon Lightning

There it was
in a dream –
three-quarter moon
flashing blue-white
lunar lightning,
warning all walkers and lovers
like a caution signal
hanging above the street.

There it appeared
behind my eyes –
trapped in its position,
thrashing in orbital constraint,
about to burst,
about to explode its man-face
all over the pavements
of the night sky.

Struck down by a slice of moonlight,
I lay curled into a crescent shape
like that lunar epileptic
reflecting on the rough and cobbled streets
of yesterday's journey –
illuminating the need for a divining rod,
a blind man's walking stick
for the next steps forward.

HOME

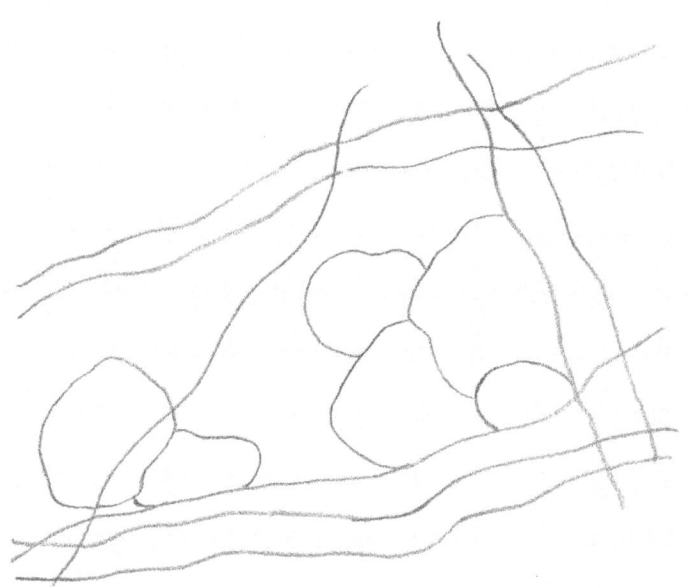

Grace Notes: (An Invitation to the West)

In some Middle Eastern tongues
the word for "rain" and "grace" are the same.

Rain invites rest,
staying inside and stoking the fires of the heart.

Rain invites dissolving
and silent waiting for re-formation.

Rain calls for courage
and the patience of those in hibernation.

Rain holds the cure
for minds distracted by the busyness of sunny days.

Rain calls for focus
on that which is ungraspable.

Rain holds out its moist hand
and invites us to do what we have never done:
to listen, for one hour, to its little melodies,
to close our eyes and step, naked, into its shower,
to stand still for five minutes, without resistance,
and feel the grace of rain.

Diving Instructions

Take one thousand years
To turn your head
Slowly to the left
Or to the right.

Relax into the "stop" --
That knot of nausea which signals entry
Into deeper waters;
A knot that has been there
In the pit of the stomach
For a long time,
Just now noticed during descent;
A knot not unlike the one
The rock balancer feels
Just before the stones align,
Defying gravity.

There is the urge to run
And resist in the old way,
To escape the unknown depths
Where we lose our minds
And feel for something else.
Disorientation fills the mouth
And thickens the tongue.
The breath moves us farther down
Like a diver's lung.
We can't fathom how this will end.

The head takes one thousand years
And twenty thousand leagues
To turn back
To center.

Note to Self: Saturday Afternoon

Your sister is at the coast
With her man;
You are at home washing clothes
And making beds;
You do not play music
But instead listen to the breeze,
The traffic, the birds,
And the occasional distant voice.

You have a glass of wine.
You look at the trees.
You think perhaps a ringing phone,
Going online, or watching TV
Would help you feel connected.
You feel the pull of that.

Yet you stop and rest here.
Quietly.
Rest here with whatever you are doing.
Feeling at ease
With mundane tasks.
Not hurrying through them just to get to the next
Seemingly better thing.
(I think I know who gave you that idea!)

Who taught you that on any lovely
Weekend afternoon
The world is full of people outside
In couples, in groups
Partying, boating, making love in the sand?
(Who in the world taught you that?)

Every kind of thing imaginable is happening
At this very moment!
In fact!

So why cling to some idea
Of how to spend your leisure;
Be glad, first of all, that you have some.
Do not pack your life to the brim.
Keep time open.
Enjoy that delicious at-home-in-my-own-skin-feeling.
What is this habitual anxiety
To be doing something else?
(And yes, I know who gave you that idea, too.)

Just breathe and taste the air.
Bask in the warmth of the light.
See what is in front of you
Without eye-grasping.
Do what your body asks of you.
Begin with rest,
And let your life unfold from here.

The Music of Release

Half-remembered dreams
Cluster through these nights,
Old themes of wandering
Lost in an urban labyrinth,
Taking the wrong road to nowhere;
Dreams of frustration, theft, flood,
Lateness, shame, confusion;
Dreams like residue on the ocean floor,
Dissolving bubbles that float up
And evaporate in the light.

Woven among the dark seaweed tangles
Are dreams of grandmothers,
Confident goddesses of calm and care,
Their wise-woman energy circling
Around and around
Spiraling and scouring spent karma,
A persistent wash of seawater,
Gathering momentum and power
Like a symphonic locomotive
With melodies for wheels.

Old dreams with their old themes
Pull carloads of burden,
Well-worn tracks of bones and joints,
Ancient steam train maneuvers
Sharp switchbacks of painful angles,
Sticky tissue and tight muscle;
The train pulses a rhythm
That cleanses the circuitry
And clears the path for a new somatic song.

Passengers, frail ghosts,
Meekly wave goodbye to the old landscapes:
The desolate fields and stagnant lakes,
The knotted limbs of broken trees
With recorded rings of stress and injury,
The sad pavements of restriction,
The crumbling houses of neglect.
They wave goodbye to the mechanics of fear
And the numbness of shock;
Goodbye to the barracks and schools
With cramped children shaking
Under wooden desks
Protecting from attack.

As morning arrives
The night train begins its final cadenza,
Sounding the three-voiced chord of a train
Trumpeting relief and resolution.

The roundhouse of the body
Plays its own music
With its own structure,
Homecoming music
That it knows by heart.

Singing by Feel

To sing a line of music,
Fly-fishing in the air,
Following the arc of the curve
Toward an ever-renewing point;

Opening the ribs,
An increase of pressure and space,
Sending the arrow from stretched bow
Toward the center of center;

Following the lead bird
In a formation of many arisings,
A gathering into one shape,
Moving fearlessly through the void;
Through darkness and light,
Through day and night,
Propelled toward the unknown,
Feeling the way,
Listening like the deaf composer
Possessed by ecstasy;

Taking aim with breath in lungs
Exhaling like a comet trailing radiance,
Cosmic baseball knocked out of the park
Into blue yonder.

SOMA SONG

Sometimes the Breath

Sometimes the breath is a bell ringing,
Tolling, calling, vibrating,
Arousing such compelling vocal release…

Sometimes the breath is a silent clapper,
Swaying to a sweet pulse,
But not striking anywhere at all,
Just rocking like a small boat
On the current of the moment…

Sometimes the breath is a candle,
A flashlight, a miner's lamp,
A penetrating flame illuminating hidden jewels
On a long beam of exhale
Tracing veins of gold…

And sometimes the breath is so still and balanced
It seems to disappear
But for a tiny trickle of inhale,
Which arrives like a surprise…

A Sentient Being Senses

What is a body?
A conveyance to carry the head around?
A duty to maintain for a few decades
Then watch with dismay as it decays and betrays?
Something to abuse, cut, and punish
For the sins of the fathers?
Something to dress up and parade about?
Something to sell for someone else's gain?
Something to feed, medicate or otherwise distract
From this moment?

A sentient being feels the flow of the silent pulse,
Hears the music that is always playing,
Moves with the smallest house of time,
And delights in the forms that arise.
Why have a body if not for this?
Why have knowledge if not for this?
All recollection, prediction, exploration and resolve--
Pointless if not for this!

A sentient being senses.
Let the body do what the body does.
Let the cells see the pour of light,
Let the scents of the world awaken senses,
Let the tastes of love anchor the mind.

A sentient being senses.

Soma Song

What is this body
With its hills and gullies,
Its smooth plains and sudden peaks,
Its grassy meadows by flowing creek,
Its forest growth and deep caverns…

What is this scent of hay,
This buzz of cricket and bee,
This drum pulse and electric current…

What is this round mass,
This rotating moon
Moving through an invisible orbit…

What galactic arms sending and extending
Into airpools of shapely space…

What legs of strength moving across the Earth
In circles and spirals of sparkle and flash…

What voices whisper secret delights
And eternal, unending joys…

What is this body
That follows God around through the heavens
Like a faithful dog
Nipping at the master's heels
Angling for a rub or a bone
To chew in holy communion
With the scent of the flesh still fresh…

What is this body ritual
Of wafer, candle, bell and wand,
This nightly incantation of love chant, sleep,
And the white dreams of mystery…

What is this body
Whose shadow can be projected
Onto the walls of the house,
Dancing concert of bright and dark,
Focus and blur,
Design and change…

What is this play, this river, this vibration
Of atomic and Adamic origins
Unfolding and unfolding forever and ever,
Atman breath of inspiration, pranayama
And pranams to all beings whose breath,
Whose eating and resting,
Whose making and undoing,
Whose time and whose ghosts
Whose pleasures and terrors,
Whose Earth is their coffin,
Whose Earth is their ovum,
Whose Earth is their breast,
Whose Earth is their fire,
Whose Earth is their food,
What is this Earth, this body?

What is this spilling of ripe flesh,
Red and sweet tomato globe of desire
And choosing the same bite over and over
For aeons sucking, drinking, tasting, swallowing,

Creating flesh,
Destroying flesh,
This living body dying daily
This cup of bitter tea…

Just This.

What is this?

What wondrous love is this, o my body, o my soul?
What wondrously woven basketry
With tattoo skin patterns carrying forward
The story and symbol of a culture,
Warp and weft neatly balanced
To dissolve itself
And re-create itself
Over and over again according to ancient instructions
Within the chromosomes…

What wondrous love is this?
What wondrous pantry, pharmacy, nursery, and garden
Of earthly delights?
What hot, tropical vacation destination,
What cruise ship of adventure,
What wondrous container, completion, return and home.
What wondrous creation wherein information flows
On a heartbeat, in a word, a touch, or in a glance.

Wondrous indeed!
Wondrous in seed, salt, lymph, bile and blood…
Wondrous heart most marvelous pump and primal throb
Of excitation responding immediately to the slightest
And smallest impulse…

Wondrous leafy bean-tree lungs
Reversing, transferring, exchanging elements
On the crest of the next inhale…

Wondrous pancreas, thin fish swimming at the center
Nearly invisible,
Bowing servant of sweetness and delicacy…

Wondrous liver that lets us live!
Wondrous kidney that discriminates and filters,
Wondrous marrow factory
Nestled within the honeycomb of bone…

Wondrous water, protein, fat, enzymes,
Collagen, gasses and glycogen,
Wondrous tubules, glands, teeth and sinew,
Wondrous hair, skin, lip and finger…

Wondrous walnut cap of brain tunnels and secretions
Lubricating synapses
And allowing movement in a millionth of a second…

Wondrous nail, nose, and knee,
Wondrous larynx, tongue, and hand,
Wondrous serpentine intestine
And all the sacs that build, move and break down
All the live-long grocery list of fuel and foolishness
We consumptives consume…

Wondrous fibroblast fibers,
Knitted scarf of connective tissue
That wraps and structures us
With the tensile strength of steel….

Wondrous white reserve guard cells
Loaded with antigen ammunition,
Power proteins that protect the nation…

Wondrous chorus line of dancing cochlear cells,
Legs high-kicking to the beat of air waves,
Rubbing electricity into a musical Morse code…

Wondrous egg cell,
Blazing sun of a thousand rays and over-easy juiciness…

Wondrous womb of warmth, fluids, and rest –
The remedy for illness is always the same:
Warmth, fluids and rest…

For be it womb or cocoon, sack, bed or pouch
We are graced with rest and quietude,
Our birthright and first crib
With built-in surround-sound…

What wondrous love is this?

Be it for the intelligence of genetic organization,
Be it for the uniqueness of a thumbprint,
Be it for the chemical reactor in the mitochondria,
For these I rejoice and rejoice again…

Be it for the suicide missions and cellular cannibalisms
That occur daily as divisions, cycles, mitosis,
Regeneration, shuffling and turnover,
For these I rejoice and rejoice again…

Be it for a state-of-the-art structure, plumbing,
Temperature regulation leaning toward solar,
Interior furnishings and décor,
Entertainment center, trash disposal system,

And worldwide web grid hook-up,
For this body, like any worthy home,
I rejoice and rejoice again…

I rejoice in all 206 bones
Strong enough to support their weight in tons…
I rejoice in the 29 vertebrae in spinal alignment
Movers and stabilizers all caressing a fine filament
That co-ordinates more information each day
Than all the telephone systems in the world…

I rejoice in neural linkages with 50,000 dendrites
Just between 2 cells!

I rejoice in the 3 pound brain with 100 billion nerve cells
Packed in like canned beans…

I rejoice in all 28 bones of the foot
Including miraculous talus, tarsals, tibia and toes,
Tiny weight lifters of renown and decoration…

I rejoice in the 30 foot laboratory and recycling plant
That turns food into energy for poetry…

I rejoice in our watery environment
And the 100 miles of blood vessels in the kidneys
Feeding a million tiny filters 2 pints per minute…

I rejoice in the 6 million red blood cells contained
In just a half ounce of blood…

I rejoice in the 24,000 breaths we take each and every day,
Moving over 400 cubic feet of air
Through millions of tiny sacs in the lungs…

I rejoice in vibrating vocal folds,
Paired hummingbird wings of the throat
Singing praises to the day…

I rejoice in swimming sperm
Clustered 200 million strong,
A tadpole navy all dressed up
And bursting with a plan…

I rejoice in the embryonic 8-celled blackberry
That we all once were before growing to infancy…

I rejoice in the miniature hammers, harps,
And balancing stones inside the ear
Giving us symphonies and an upright orientation…

And I rejoice in the bread-loaf maze that is the optic nerve,
The corneal striations and retinal road map
Of our open, amazed eyes
That bring light into this body,
That let us see clearly
This somatic starship of flesh and translucence,
Spinning through space,
Yet completely
And utterly
And always
At Home.

With Thanks……..

I offer huge armloads of gratitude to Ron Pickup for his editorial wisdom and astute suggestions; to Alaskan writer Carol Ford whose great generosity and keen eye (after all, she comes from Kenai) was of immense help during the final stages of preparation for publication; and to mic harper for her warm-hearted and gentle approach to craft and intention. You all made the months of chiseling and sculpting a richly creative process. Gratitude also to all the colleagues, friends and family that gave a listening ear, often to newborn first drafts! My thanks to Susan Wenger, Judy Stoltenberg, Vlatka Varga, Janaka, and my beloved sister, Judy, who has been there through it all.

And deepest bows to the Word Project Press team, especially Gillian Herbert and Patricia Harrelson, for their kind and supportive steering and cheering.

Joy Willow's three great loves are poetry, painting, and piano improvisation. Academic training includes a B.A., and M.A. in English, as well as post-graduate work in music at Temple University. Passionate about teaching, she formerly taught community college English, and has continued to teach voice and piano privately for the past 30 years. Joy is also an abstract naturalist painter. She enjoys moving from words to paint to sounds, as each medium inspires the other.

Joy lives in the Sierra foothills of Northern California in Mother Lode country among the woodland oaks and the spirits of ancient tribal dwellers.

www.ingramcontent.com/pod-product-compliance
Lightning Source LLC
Chambersburg PA
CBHW020916090426
42736CB00008B/655